PHILIP FINKLE

# DOUBTS
## and
# REDOUBTS

## Selected Poems

iUniverse, Inc.

New York   Bloomington

# DOUBTS and REDOUBTS
## Selected Poems

*iUniverse books may be ordered through booksellers or by contacting:*

*iUniverse*
*1663 Liberty Drive*
*Bloomington, IN 47403*
*www.iuniverse.com*
*1-800-Authors (1-800-288-4677)*

*ISBN: 978-1-4401-3644-3 (pbk)*
*ISBN: 978-1-4401-3645-0 (ebk)*

*Printed in the United States of America*
*iUniverse rev. date: 4/23/09*

*It is on disaster that good fortune perches;*
*It is beneath good fortune that disaster crouches.*

*- Tao Te Ching*

Oh, I went to the city
And there I did weep –
Men a-crowin' like asses
And livin' like sheep.

- Kenneth Patchen

# OUTLAW'S DIRGE

Im tombstone cities where gals ain't pretties,
Old Billy DeLyon had kettled his fishes.
He reined up at the hitching post
And tossed away his last sad ghost.
His past was all a cancerous sore,
His mind a fester, his heart a whore –
All filled with rusty beercan smiles
And hangdog eyes and bleeding piles.
He panted his last and goddamed all his wishes,
In tortured alleys where friends ain't palies.

(1970)

# IN HER SAD FOREST

I know she has many colored boxes,
and each has comical teardrops in it –
teardrops that laugh all down her cheeks and drop
softly to the cushioned ground where her feet
tread through the multi-colored leaves that are
happy to die and glad to imbibe her
tears, since even the forest floor knows that
one of the shining ones is passing there.

(1970)

## HIS SISTER, AURORA BOREALIS

They'd roomed in the same womb
and talked at night in gladiator tombs,
until the public's thorny finger plucked out his eye
and rinsed it off in a stream of sorrows.
    His screams were her tears,
    all in the family of man,
    as her asphodel breasts had tasted his mushroom ears.
        she nursed him in the sewers of the city
        while the serpents slept,
        (the moon tolled,
        the sun listened)
        feet glistening,
        and only nursemaids danced in the graveyards.
            He molted and blanched,
            eating only plums and lizard waxings,
            short of breath and long of heart,
            stirring in the cauldron's endless stew,
            totalling the wins and losses of his dogs.
She thought that he was recovering
and stepped out to test the evening's heir,
apparently now knowing
(since he died in her abscence)
that he was a rainbow.

(1970)

3

# NIGHTSONG

They hide from the daylight
    but at night my pendular moods
        steal slowly from the underbrush of my dreams
            and pounce
                with cat's dead-aim intent.
Tactics of evasion have failed
    and my twilight strength deserts me,
        but not you –
           at the lowest
              as at the highest
                  you are there:
                      constant cohort of my shadows
                        and empress of the dark –
                          the cup for my haunted fluid.

So this is you the next time –
    the time we always knew would be
        but perhaps never believed
            (there have always been so many too few
                and the hope of them so painful).
Cyclical kisses from  your metaphysical mouth

empty my nightmares –
    your eyes rekindling
        to drive the succubus skittering
        as we begin again.
Now you and I
    count high in the endless flesh of dreams.

(1971)

# MORNING SHOWER

She's a cloudburst
and her beansprout fingers
leave me limp and damp
on this freshly wet smelling morning
dew dazzled
as she taps out the calculus
of loving
on the sweating temples of
my drought withered mind.

(1971)

# EMPTY RETURN

Both you and the sun-
light are there as one
in the waiting door-
way to see if more
than just empty cof-
fins are taken off
the night train. Indef-
inite, as in ref-
erence to some gone
love who's become pawn
instead of knight, tear-
drops plead to no ear.

(1971)

# CAMPGROUND

In the deserts of her abscence
 i huddled on the sacred grounds
  discussing Nietzche
   with the spirit of Mangas Coloradas,
    his flinty eyes flinging campfires
   from cheekbones leathered by his vigil –
  and when he faded
 ran war-whooping through the Catalinas
  to swim the sands of Cañon del Oro
   with the heart of *El Lobo*
    wounded by the brave,
     trailing blood theough the mesquite,
     parched and limping
      but pushing on
     with the strength of those who
know
    that the wound is only mortal.

         (1971)

# TOO QUICK

1

Omphaloskepsis
Takes such years of long practice:
Spider's sad matrix.

2

Not to be alone –
        Almost a simple feeling
        of flesh clutching bone.

(1971)

# UNPOEM

An unpoem has
  no rhyme
      nor reason ore
any grammar either
        or it wouldn't be
                    one, un
            that it Its
        .punctuation
            don't help anything
                        can be a mess but
            only a lot of things
        Are unpoems
                    or are they or us
                            either
            Every thing and everybody may
                somehow be a poem
                    someday rather than
                        an unpoem?

(1971)

# DAYBREAK

At the dawning of our new daze all of the middleminds were shuffling their fats and indexing their little cardthoughts.

Technical waves washed the shore white, lily-white, death-white, gone-white,

And tubers sprouted in the arid sands of deserted lands of pallid ancestry.

Rulers of past heraldry dryly doffed hats of crimsom to tarnished ladies.

And the winds howled: the humming winds of desolate things,

While miserly maidens picked sad blooms from the misery bush and empty hands grasped the morning's throat.

Mourning doves wobbled through thoughtless forests in search of good deeds for the rejected trees.

And yet the sprouts of Burlington and Buena Vista waved their tattered pennants in hope of due penance,

For all of the teary ones had since long departed to relatives of the storm,

And orphans adrift were aparted, alerted by the cries of
   dying beeches and able spruces of warlock pride.

The enchanted woodlands, being spritely attired, retried
   returning wards.

Hordes of the sickcast beached ahead on the palsied
   shoreline, trailing smoke thoughts.

And yet, and yet, our words grew dim and he who wasted
   wanted not,

For tiny knots and clusters of starshapes had accrued in
   the abscence of misdeeds,

And strong steeds galloped past the rising sons of Sun's
   house in skies of glory,

And the purple haze of done victories retreated before the
   bright clawing of forgiveness.

Redress of addled dreams seems softly now,

And we must come together.

   And we must come together.

                                                    (1972)

# YOU CAN BE IN MY RENAISSANCE IF I CAN FROLIC THROUGH YOUR GOLDEN EARS

American Cult sure
        is a watchglass culture:
     Bacteria minds
           in
             molecular beds:
  Not even the dead
       are so often misled
         As a mind that just wandered
            off
                 down
            some rose prime path
              to
             It's dust:
               Reward.

                    (1972)

Philip Finkle

# HIGH SPEED WOMEN

High speed women will be a death to you.
    They'll steal your breath away,
        They never will delay –
            They ride into your heartroom
                on high-test iron horses
                  And
                      kick around all your
                          fought-for trophies
                              with their big motor-
cycle boots.

They burn your mind in no time
    and flash off into the no where
        to leave you with ashes
                on your hands.
High speed women haul their own
    but run too fast to climb
        and haven't any time
                to waste fondling pansies
        when they can easierly roll their own.

(1972)

# EVERYDAY LADY

She is only ordinary
        as the scent of rain
               or a small child's smile.
She promises no castles,
        no jewelled daggers,
           no moneyed thrones –
    she only touches softly
        and warms each night's respite.
  She wears no flowers
              in her hair,
    she promises no dreams,
        she draws no maps for golden years,
           she's only what she seems:
    Neither monarch nor gypsy temptress,
        no nymph,
             no ephemeral spell;
        no summer's maiden,
              no siren's call;
        she's only each moment's all.
She is not extraordinary,
        there's no divine dung near,
  Only the sound of life's breath:
        rhythmic partner at my ear.

               (1972)

# JINGLE IN PLAIN DREAD

William Bonney,

our bonnie we lad,

you've infected us all

with the sickness you had.

(It was six-guns

and tombs,

now its syringes

and zombies.)


A social outcast

is now at the door –

Is it Ricky Rockstar

or a death-dealing whore?

There is doom and destruction

dripping down off your chin,

and the look in your eyes

is again and again.

Are you Chuck,

the mad rapist,

or Shiva,

my friend?

Mother Kali
     has suckled
          both warriors
              and saviors
   and Ms. Liberty
         gave us all
            strange new behaviors.

A rhyme
     for our time
         is Mysterious variable;
   Breath
       equals
         Death,
           a most modern parable.

Oh Billy,
     you're leading us
         on to the fray
         And we fear the cruel journey
           but remember the way.

               (1972)

# IN MY PRIME

From off the top it came one night
"You're in your prime,"

she said.

She meant to speak of lusty things

she did

I heard

I hid.

Just old enough to know something

Yet young enough to use it

Compelled enough to risk it all

Resolved enough to lose it.

In my prime –

that's in my time,

not of it.

Before design,

after my crime

but not above it.

I came on stage

clothed in just words,

post-entrance

and pre-exit.

"I'll repeat this only once,"

I said,

resplendent

and redundant.

And then I breathed

and lunged

and heaved

and shoved myself

r i g h t

past me.

"where am i now?"

I asked

she smiled

I knew

I'd passed it.

(1972)

# THERE'S ONE BORN EVERY MINUTE

The ravagers of the earth
  are sending out men in slick blue suits
    to wholesale fire
      as a sure cure "fer what ails ya"
        and every Discount Decadence store
       will carry six brands of pox americana
      in color-coordinated polystyrene containers
        ("one shot and you're cool all yuga")
          in fact, you're ice
         And ice that desires fire
       is quick like praying mantis
      and slow like tick of the clock
     And the road to mind-nova
      is littered with the burned hulls
        of night-ship souls
      that move in moth-sure silence
  to the sky-flame brilliance of burning cities.

            (1974)

# WOMAN

In this age of storms
> you are servant of the wind
>> and I,
>>> the vassal of thunder.
You are as the wheel of turning seasons –
> your colors shift
>> and your shapes are melting.
>>> I am the rain of the morning,
>>>> You are the vessel of evening –
> we are dissolving into a starswirl
>> of sweet light
>>> sleeping on the tongue of the dreamer.
I can feel the forms changing now;
> the names are all reordered –
>> Speaking your true name
>>>> scatters the demons of doubt
And
> you must be the pool of endless depth;
>> I must be the stone of constant dropping.

(1975)

# SURVIVORS

Few survive here
   and, if any,
      fewer thrive
 Here
   at the leading edge
                  of night
   where dawn
            seems furthest
      and the harvest
               is meager
      and the wordsmiths
         are most eager
                  to speak
            of a woman who talks with fire
            and a bird that rises
                  from rivers
            and batters at the windows
               of this world.

(1976)

# CANTO MODERNO DE LOS YANQUIS

Now the children of greed
    seek a creed
        to lead through starless nights
            of heaven-thunder to come,
And the horsemen of avarice
            still ride here,
      midst crumbling hydrocarbon empires
And they bring the long cloak of night
        with the cold of their calculations –
O, armsmaker to the world
    you are a smelting pot
      but cauldrons bubble over –
            Mammon!


Enough of:
    "From each according to his audacity,
        To each according to his greed."
Time for:
      "From each according to his tranquilities,
        To each according to his deed."


Through god's eye

we must sail

with a peaceful cry

for the heavens.

No cocksure musket-clutcher

needed now –

not here

In this place of

not wholly holy endeavor.

Leave

your disease

at the door,

señor.

Man-sized technology –

magic Tortoise!

Revolutionary turn of the wheel –

Run Coyote!

(1979)

# MONEY TALKS

Money talks.

It says,
    "Money is power, pal –
        Show me a featherless biped
            and I'll show you an easy mark."

It says,
    "Kick your shoes off, cousin,
    Put your feet up,
    Let me make you a deal you Can't refuse,
    I mean *thou shalt not reject* this offer, pilgrim!
        "Peddle your cratered soul for
            a half-a-dream's worth of synapse juice!
                (You central-nervous-system-types
                    tend strongly to the tyrannical.)"

It says,
    "You want to see something sister?
    I'm talking the grease the squeaky one gets,
    The brew the bankers stir,

The veritable lubricious pelf that powers the drummer,
The specie that soothes the whir of the gears of com-
merce."

It says,
    "This wealth shines brightly, buster,
    Fueled by the flames of burning 'fossil-love' –
    'Fossil-love' sapped by the drills of the
                power-suckers,
                power-liners,
                main-liners,
                hard-liners,
    and possibly-just-a-few-lines-left-creatures
    slouching towards the Southgate Shopping Mall."

Money talks.
    It doesn't listen.
        It never learns –
            "'Power as a gift of the life force',
                Use it wisely little pennymonger,
                    For there are bigger things a-brew,
                        Yes, far bigger things than you."

                            (1980)

# MANSONG

## I.

Inertia is the seed of longing
  Boundless light is at the heart of silence
    Silence is preserver of pure powers
        - pure powers
                are creators of balance
        And
                balance is the sound
                        of dragonfly wings:
                a song of breath
                    over seas of shadow –
                the flow
                        is one way
                            and many

## II.

Song is signature
  Time is the rhythym of matter
        Matter is the figure of the instant
        The mark of the fire-tamer

is on the face of the hour

And

the flower of flesh

blossoms

in dreams

of smoke-fleshed singers

whose firesongs

write godspark

across the sky –

Song rings

from the anvil

of meat


III.


The partial craves the whole


There is no name for the true one


There are many names

for the many sons of One


Spark envisions fire

and true spirits

dance circles –

The heart is a lantern:

its light

flares in the eyes

of the corporeal engine

as

ebb

seeks

flow

IV.

The leanest line

is

the thin edge

of song

carving name

from nightstone

The sharpest blade

is the thin edge

of manheart

where

love and hate

are joined

in the seared lips

of time's kiss

The truest song

flies straight to the earthheart


V.


Song

is the prey of spirit

and each spirit

draws strength

for its flight

from its tribal song

And

All the songs of all the tribes

together

sounds the song

that stirs the dreams

of true singers

and long dreamers


The song

of the people

rides the night wind


VI.


Spirit

is

    Fire

        fed by a voice that speaks through all men:

           its timbre

              is fuel for beads of fire-lace

                strung on a necklace of

                      night

                and the solitary hunter

                is stalking

                      white flame

            with which to spell the name

                    of the wondrous


        Change

            is a child

                of the clock


## VII.


The blade at the throat of mind

        has been honed

           on the many wars of this one world

  Spider gods sit hunched

        at a fire of flesh

          hungry for vision:

                A cast of hawks!

The hunter knows killing
      locus is focus
  and inhumanity
           is human
The locust hordes
  and winged lords
    all hover
        at the heat of finity

Dust sailors!
  Try all edges of the heart
    but
       *cling*
        to the center
There are streams within streams
    and
      rivers in rivers

Water is the first home
  and the virtues of water
    dwell at the base of all homes
Cast loose
    on seasons of sorrow
        gravity pulls at the root of the flow

And straight to the source flies spirit.

(1980)

# WHOOP

Hold on,
> man is coming.
> Hold on,
>> new man is coming!
> Hold on,
>> threatened lives of earth,
>>> speechless trees, hope-seeking children,
>>>> rain in search of good ground,
>>>>> parched     masses,     crushed

classes –
>> we are all one class;
>>> seeds of the earth mother.
>> Let man nourish earth
>>> as earth has nourished man.


Hold on,
> my countrymen,
>> 'tis of thee, powered by thy entropy
> I sing:
>> How many no's don't make a was,
>>> how many ifs a why?

Hold the low ground for ours, my friend,
It's onward we must try –
But trees grow big while men grow small,
and touch don't feel and words don't mean –
And cardboard cowboys ride the range
while angeltramps grow lean.

(1981)

# DIALOGUE

I heard the last philosopher say,

    "All we're talking about is

        what we're using to talk about it with, i.e.,

            what we use to say what we mean is what we

mean."

    But tell me all about the things

        that they don't discuss at the Country Club.

    "watch......watch,

        they let the world into the hands of evil men."

        why are they enlisting masters of torture?

    Give us another war criminal to throw out the first

pitch!

I heard the next-to-the-last poet say,

    "Noble Man –

        o smoke-maker, whale-killer, seed-sower, scourge

of rainforests,

            took-maker, desert-spreader, space-voyager,

earth-ruler:

    Your greatest adversary is yet yourself."

    Man: Highly knowledgeable, mildly intelligent life

form.

    Earth: A finite hope.

The union of these two is history:

Man feeds on lower species.

Why shouldn't men be consumed?

The pendulum swings

but always from a later location.

The equation of evolution

narrows and opens.

(1981)

# SEVEN ANGELS OF DESTRUCTION
# AND A WHISPER OF HOPE

The first angel of destruction waved a flag and shouted,
    "Gentlemen,
        start your infernal combustion engines!"

The second angel of destruction observed,
    "You want the good things
      when the truly good things are
        not-to-be-had-things."

The third angel of destruction said,
    "Give me your toxic waste,
    your fall-out,
        your poisons –
      I'll mix you a mutant brew
      to singe the evil
        from your offspring."

The fourth angel of destruction
    packed his covenants and alliances
      in the sacred ditty bag

sewn of clouds,
lined with the tears of
barren earthlings.
Raped landscapes
burned in his eyes
And plumes of
sulfur dioxide
trailed in his wake
as he laughed all the way
to the gates of Babylon.

Meanwhile,
the fifth angel of destruction
led the slaves of money-economics
to high financial flames.

And the sixth angel of destruction
wore robes of light
and the sandals of a fisherman
and wanted not to bring wailing
and so walked silently
from the city of doom.

And the seventh angel of destruction
had tears in her eyes,
her immortality drooped

about her shoulders,
and with head down
she trod from the presence of man.


The whisper of hope
breathed its last breath
into man's ear,
Speak with angels yet


while you may."


(1981)

# LOVE IS A VELVET CHAIN

On the journey to the markets
 we've met at the crossroads of cunning
  and there lies a velvet chain.
      And among the oaks and sycamores,
        along the ridge of pines –
  You are a forest
            full of wild things,
      And I am a blundering pioneer.


There are wrens and robins;
 there are moles and squirrels
  and hawks and crayfish
    and catfish and barley,
      milkweed and daisies
    and the names are myriad.
        (You,
              the ocean of memory;
      I,
              the molecule of desire.)


I've wandered from the road to ruin;
 our eyes have met

on a narrow path
   through clover and foxtail
      and ants and bees
      and a cast of hawks
         circling high
                     overhead.
woman is possibility.
      man is expectation.

                     (1981)

# GONER'S RAG

what you gonna do when the fire starts?
  what you gonna do when its flamin'?
when you call for help my friend,
  who you gonna be namin'?

where you gonna keep your valuables, ma'm,
  Through lightning and through thunder?
who gonna help you rise above?
  what gonna drag you under?

How you gonna pay when the man collects?
  what's it take to buy you?
where you gonna keep the things you know
  when the things you don't fly by you?

what you gonna use to fight off lions?
  what to scare the danger?
what colors will you finally fly,
  when you meet that last sad stranger?

(1982)

# DIATRIBE

"My young men shall never work.
Men who work cannot dream,
and wisdom comes in dreams.
You ask me to plow the ground.
Shall I take a knife and tear
my Mother's breast?
Then when I die,
She will not take me
to her bosom to rest.
You ask me to dig for stones.
Shall I dig under her skin
for bones?
Then when I die,
I canot enter her body
to be born again.
You ask me to cut grass
and make hay and sell it,
and be rich like white men.
But how dare I cut off
my Mother's hair?
All the dead men will
come to life again.

we must wait here in the
house of our Fathers
and be ready to meet him
in the body of our Mother."

- Smohalla


Technonarcosis!
stoned crazy on technology:
tool of fools
and stick of sages.
Machines, even of doom,
are not evil;
It is their masters who must answer.
Political harangues for the ethics of convenience –
A cacophony of voices
raised in rhyme of ruin
rises on crest of fire.
Evil technologies
are not of the new age;
They are of a dead age.
Look to their logos
to judge them
in this age of transition
when men of mean spirit

still shackle earth.

Man's strength lies in numbers
(community of spirits).
Man's weakness lies in numbers
(army of destruction).
And they found power in a poisonous seed
which grew into nuclear devices
and horrible excretions
and finally deletions.
Species at the mercy of man,
Take heed!


You have nothing to win but your genes!
Your existence!
Beware
the author of extinction!
Take care –
the thief of your mission.
Races at the mercy of man,
Look out!
Buffalo Bill
has poisons and powers.


"A nation founded on genocide,
built with slavery –
Now ravenous for parking lots."

Stay clear of acquisitive men:
They have no honor –
And a man without honor
has nothing.

Man is known by name.

Name is the sum of a life's actions.

(1982)

# REPORT TO THE FISHERMAN

It was the fattest of times,
          It was the leanest of times.
   It was the serenest of times,
            It was the meanest of times.
For the Few there was more of the Bounty
   For the Many there was less of the Plenty.
El Dorado lay down with the Sheik's concubines
   and woke up hungry.
Their gods were of metal and fire,
    and they worshipped them
             to the point of exhaustion:
      A selfish, short-sighted, hedonistic,
          hell-bent-for-leather group
            barreling   down   the
cut-off to Hell,
    no exit,
   no deposit,
  no return,
  no shit.
       O arrogance of power,
         crash of great opulent towers,

rotted at the cores,

whores of power politics

and executions in the night.

Ah, the flickering lights of Gehenna:

How inviting;

But here,

another automobile-orphan,

and there,

    another war-orphan,

Lord,

    there are so many.

"Only the young die good,"

    the torturer said.


What comes after?

  what restores laughter?

    we don't need a revolution.

      we need a reconstitution of values –

      of course

        that will probably take a revolution.

(1984)

# TELLURIC ETUDE #1

The first new man
  hoped to be the last lethal man,
      But he hasn't been yet –
          For there on the tossing deck
              stood the oppressor:
                  high-tech eyes aglitter,
                      armed to the teeth,
                          beweaponed and bewitched,
                  while the crew cowered befuddledly
                          in the background.
The hemispheric blood trail
          seems to lead to the Octopus.
      (The other hemisphere
              of course has its Squid.)


It's the yin and the yang of it,
once you get the hang of it,
          globally speaking.
      But once you get the hang of it,
              Dang if it don't change shape –
                  The two are one
                              in the Mother.
                      Circle turn,
                          And life take cover!

                                  (1984)

49

# TELLURIC ETUDE #2

"Education begins with poetry."

- Confucius

Poetry begins in mystery;
  There was more yesterday
    But still there are some riddles
      here left for you to solve,
          tiny earth crawler.
    Their answers may astound you,
        or surround you,
      or elude you or preclude you,
       or debase you or erase you.
At a point in your evolutionary education,
  You will learn betrayal.
  At a time of reconciliation
    there will be a singing of songs
        and a righting of wrongs.
  And we,
    already hot under the jewelled collar,
 we,
    of the grossest national product,

*exportatum imperialis* –

we gaze intently at the screen

As the media master gets mixed reviews.

News headlines read:

"Space Conqueror Conquered by Time."

*Tempus Finit.*

(1985)

# TELLURIC ETUDE #3

The Full Cold Moon,
    longest, darkest night of winter;
        Thirteenth daughter of the moon –
            Ten pairs of tortoises cannot oppose you.


Man holds sway by the powers of mirrors and clocks
    And Hollywood fantasies:
        the face of Colossus,
            worshipping youth, beauty, wealth and plea-
sure
                (one necessity and three diversions) –
Fast food commercials and video circuses for the masses.
    In the days of classes
        monochromatic mentalities
            dichotomize realities
                into black and white disasters,
        Only flickers of humanity
            glimmered in our primitive minds
        And as we grew older,
    realizing the exponential nature of our dilemma,
        we learned to nod our heads

as though we'd known all along
what the score was.
Great techno-industrial dinosaurs of doom
crashed through our nightmares,
Songs of self-destruction whistling in our ears,
The wanton ways of wealth winning
when we're losing all the while –
The arrogant shall not inherit the earth
or they shall despoil it.
Super Powers come and go,
posing for Grosz and Picasso.

(1985)

# TELLURIC ETUDE #4

One lingering Eve
whose arts were all sciences,
Opened an Americanadam's eyes,
Never to stay closed again.
And now that no innocence remains
in this unnatural state of affairs
to which we've attained;
How to regain
that state now rare?
How to restore those rains descending:
those rains both fruitful and unending?
On the right shines Lord Shiva, ascendant –
No one reads any rights to defendants;
On the left glows his consort, aflame –
No one remembers his own name.
It's a shakedown for survival:
Could be curtains or dawn resplendant:
Final casting for the species –
Could be whipped cream, could be feces.
whatever the outcome,
we must not wait on god

but find the god within us.

Earth sings only for its descendants –

    Sings,

        "Live for the benefit of all beings."

        (what is man without context?)

Incants,

Oh ye of great media-power,

    Controller of airwaves –

        Mind-bender,

           Spirit-breaker:

    Oh rich rulers of things

            and men-for-now,

        Ye of much plunder,

          Ye must go under –

            for the sake of

              we, your brother's seed.

For you see we are each an attempt

    to show the way to man,

        the new way

           from today to tomorrow,

              from old to new man,

                from woman to all-

man. . .

    Though we've lived with worse,

              why should we?

It is too far down this technoillogical road

to turn back –

we must face the demon,

    wrestle him at least to a draw –

        Better yet

           Break his spine

                in ¾ time

                (slay the crew)

Then just onward,

      straight and true!

           (1986)

# TELLURIC ETUDE #5

Because we're out here on the edge,
        risking more than just destruction,
    we seem to think that all of our principles
                        should draw interest
        As if it were a huge surprise that
                matters of power politics
                        finally deal down to dollars
                                (not heaven scents)
        Has technology so confused us that
        we can no longer tell natural from unnatural –


In time of plenty
                and place of plenty
        Too much plenty
                doesn't always add up to enough plenty
                        for times of not enough –
        Yay, even unto spiritual famine!
    Sons of Cortez brought tobacco cultivation to
        the Islands and mining to the Masses.
    Sons of Willy Loman come to the Colonies
        peddling coca schemes and toxic waste scams.
But body-wise and soul-valiant,

(like the Great Blue Heron)
Garuda lifts off the Pachamama,
  bearing both Sun and Moon:
        both Reason and Spirit
            with which to reseed the races.


"Green, green
        are my true love's eyes
        and edible her hair.
Long, long
        is my true love's gaze
    and terrible her rage –
        her smile is a house in time.
            She has many facets.
                All her assets are liquid.
                  She confers my drift.
                white are her robes in winter,
                    hawkward does she rise.
                Her thighs are dexterious,
                    her fingers are most wise.
Think of morality as her kiss."


(1988)

# TELLURIC ETUDE #6

"watch your close friend, baby –
Then your enemies can't do you no harm."

- Robert Johnson


The young ones catch the scent of doom dribbling
        from the jaws of the mechanized, militarized,
     automated, man-planned, self-serving, extinction-
dealing,
          nuclear-propelled, toxic Karma-Crusher.
                Pestilence and pillage
                     have come to the global village –
                          televised to galactic gawkers.
     Presidential spokesmen stride into briefing rooms
             with lies dripping from their blood-splattered
galoshes.
          "Oh my gosh!"'s
                are the order of the day.
     Ecotastrophes on the evening news are now old hat
       as we whiz past warning signs,
             assenting to exploitative designs.
     Cult of the individual quickly becomes cult of celebrity,
             when all the while

the future is the search for community
(in its multitudinous possibilities).
There is a time of excess,
then its over.
Is that clatter of matter the unexpected days of peace
approaching?
Or the hooves of the Beast Oncoming?
"Baraka,
don't fail me now," sing the chosen.
The revolution is of course international:
adaptation
from nation to nation
till nations make no sense.
The revolution will not be what you expect,
Come comrades –
In the end it won't hurt a bit
Just to twist the head off of the exploiting insect
feeding in our gut.
No more madmen at the wheel!
We need an Idea
not a man.
Men are so small
and time is so short.

(1987)

# WITHOUT PROGRESS

There is no season for love, my love;
  There is no reason for time –
      There is a rhythym that binds us here,
          though yours may not be mine.
      Prayers may not be answered now;
         Fortunes entangle, untwine.

Autumn dogs summer
      as you, constant, stalk my heart.
  Keepers and sleepers arise for the call:
        This temporary stage is mine.
      It's a slow, slow dance we're doing, love,
        in this short, short span we stride.

You've been teaching bingo strategy to the very confused;
  I paint teardrops on the faces on postage stamps –
      There are innumerable ways to skin a cat,
        but practically none to like it.

I have learned to sleep with my hands in my pockets.
  You have learned to live with your heart in a locket.

(1987)

61

# TO A MOUNTAIN BARTENDER

The juncos have arrived
    with the conviction of winter.
  They chatter of Canadian adventures
     while Northern storms track them to the
                Colorado Rockies.
This is a proper time for dust
             to rejoin dust –
 Before the stare of death
    freezes to sheer ice.
whatever part of you can escape
    will slowly accrue to the landscape.
   Your gesture now will be
     the flicker of the yellowing aspen
       and the wave of long mountain grasses:
         Death being graduation
             to a voiceless realm.
So let us hoist a glass
    in the presence of our final host –
  that dark silent stranger at the end of the bar,
             naturally.
    we cannot discern his shrouded features.

It's as if he stands in a mist.

Yet

Here's to the one who served the brew

that helps us momentarily forget

that last appointment we must keep.

"Bartender!

Drinks all 'round!"

(1987, Idaho Springs, Colorado)

# SAINT AGONY AWAKES

The Dog Star rose at the hot breath of dawn.

All the plump complacent burghers strode out on the morn.

The Department of Marketing had designed

a cool blue package in which to wrap the destruction of the earth.

The suits were playing it heavy on the executive:

Wave after wave of hubris washed over them.

On TV the latest flesh blossoms parade past

in the least possible sunwear,

peddling breakfast cereals, automobiles and

the latest fashionable illusions,

while pale old men are driving Earth to death.

Good grass helped to pass the wars that never ended.

Bad dope killed hope, born naked in winter.

"Learn fast or lose, hot shot"

is the wisdom the streets spoke.

Country meets City,

having been slickered too long.

Balding, pot-bellied, manicured braggarts

boasted and toasted their big deals.
"There are markets out there to be developed,"
they squealed.
Your television and your newspaper lie to you
just as you wish:
"The death squads are nothing to do with us."
Now there are prophets by the dozens,
Punk pariahs and false messiahs by the score.
"This year's cause is next year's reason.
(Last year's pause is this year's treason.)"
The media crave cataclysm and soap opera;
if they cannot find them, they manufacture them.
"Tragedy in a teacup,
for your boring afternoon's enjoyment, milady."
The Queen has found a solution:
She's sent all her warriors to war,
her peasants to planting,
her ministers to meetings:
confabulations of hysterical relations
and cross-postulations of posterity.
Bad Pre
pried scales from the eyes of poverty's child.
Soon shall come again a time for snakes to sleep.
we must be peasants of purpose,
though rulers of the sky
(the best ruler rules least).

The senators can only think of colonizing the Moon.
Let us discuss the children.
And still you stand there,
like some modern anti-Noah,
ushering last pairs of various species on board
the Titan Ship *Dominion*,
piloted by transnational pirates,
their precious cargo ballasted
with fissionable waste.
They push growth to the maximum profit.
"Damn the Cautions!
All ships ahead full!"

(1988)

# BLACK CROW BLUES

Black crow, red sun.
  Begin as two, end as one.


I remember your lace curtains,
  I believed your lying eyes.
I felt you always there beside me.
  I woke up inside your sighs.
        I don't know if I've been cheated,
            I don't care if I've been blind.
        I just want to hear your laughter
            echo down the walls of time.


Grey sky, brown ground.
  Rain falls with vegetal sound.


I can't forget the lips you had then,
  I can't remember what words they said.
I never knew where your gypsy wants led.
  We're all just becoming "has-beens"
                right up to the moment that we end.
  I don't care which way the creek flows,
        I've punched my ticket to the end.

I only know what the phoebe tells me:
    There's true religion 'round the bend!

Loving thighs, nurturing breasts.
I'm a question, you're the quest.

You put a candle in the window,
  when I was no more than a thief.
     when I was thirsty without water,
       You offered me relief.
  My mind's at the cleaner's, my soul's a misdemeanor.
    Your heart's now surrounded by a fence of finest
mesh.
     I may have trashed all your wordy goodlies
         till they weren't worth a lousy
dime.
     But I always cherished your perishing flesh.

Morning thrush, evening swallow.
  Night falls, day follows.

(1988)

# LOVE AND POLITICS IN AN AGE OF UNREASON

So it is
  And so it never shall be.
    The verities are all contingencies.
  Fox crossing the ice listens for cracks of doom
    while we get our political opinions
                    from comic strips.
        The libertines all insist
                  that they're libertarians.
              The rightists claim the cloak
of the righteous.
              The masses are convinced they're
the middle classes
                  (it says so on TV everyday).
        The petty bourgeoise dance the nights away
                  in the halls of the
working poor.
          North of the border
                    sex is in your head,
        South of the border
                  politics can make you dead.

From a supine position of superiority
the ruler of sexual politics calls the play,
while some stand-up comic tells us what to dispar-
age:

politics,

celebrity,

carnality,

religion,
the Earth.

Nothing is serious.
We must be delirious.
If what I know now
were what I knew then,
I might have known why
but never'd have guessed when.


Exchanging social inanities at the reception,
Deceptions surpassed all cherished expectations.
Most of the guests were grossly overweight;
All of their humor was desperately thin.
(Cupidity overrules all other consider-
ations in this club.)
The government's duplicitous accountants
huddle with the political scriptwriters
to decide what story

the cooked books should tell.
The double face of colossus again masquerades
  as the beloved tweedle two party system –
      preserver of status pros and profit quotas.
The big money boys
      just keep shuffling the shells.
          It's a game they play so well.
              so it was then
                  And so it may be:
                      Now we must end
                          Or now they must kneel.

(1988)

# MEDICINE TALE

Kiowa woman –
 you have stepped outside the hoop.
  Did you trade all of your ponies
            for this pick-up?
  What are you searching for
            here in the white man's city?
   Was your grandfather not pulled under
            the Whiskey River?
    And now there are many more drugs to
enchain you.
      The forces of decadence crave meat and metal.
      Occasional presents become permanent pasts
            (love seldom lasts).
       Market-wise and profoundly ghoulish,
      Every nightrider wants to touch your magic.
      Now you've learned the steps
            but the steps have changed:
            The dance you're mastered
has been rearranged.
 In crazy dreams of modern robot romance, here we
come again:

always extremist in pursuit of profit or pleasure –
we lie entwined like exhausted contestants
for the title of "world's Greatest Consumer",
while some realist explains,
"Money's thicker than love,
words more slippery than blood."
And you can't throw fastballs all day long,
Though the covetous chorus sings,
"we want roses for nothing."
All of the best thoughts have been thought,
But few actions have been taken.
Though no promises were made,
All the best words have been spoken.
All of the smoke's best intentions
Are but the fire's trail of desire.
Wealthy scavengers eye the earth-jugular,
while owl-priests grow restless
in the shrinking jungles.
So *bruja* to *brujo* –
let us compare half-breed views:
what future-tense-species
awaits a word from your lips?
(You can't trick the trickster.)
who will plant the circle?
All of the warriors have become worriers:
what's a man to do?

In the present realm

        ownership is the ultimate illu-
sion.

   In the kingdom we dreamed of,

      humans had the unfenced beauty and endurance

           of yarrow, goldenrod,

        Indian paintbrush,

             musk thistle. . . . .

once loveless as a prime number,

    Now you have flesh like a feral logarithm

        and eyes eloquent as a corpse.

                (1988)

# FRIEND, LOVER, AND STILL LIFE

Oh it was beneath a gibbous moon,
    I could feel her powers waxing.
we sat and talked through the wine that night,
        my grip on reality relaxing.
Cold and bitter as the solstice
    you strode into town with both breasts blazing,
        but you let your guard down
    And I was entranced by the-most-beautiful-
woman-of-my-dreams
           of indeterminate nationality,
      only to awake in the morning to find
        that she had monkey feet!
The night New York went bust
    You said that everybody was so busy
           looking for an angle
       that nobody could see straight.
   "knowledge doubles every five years now,"
         said the Academician.
    "not fast enough,"
        replied the geneticists.
The late worm outsmarts the early bird.

I thought it was a New Day!

(It even said so in a rock 'n roll magazine.)

The ancient elements battled the modern elements:

Fire vs. Hydrogen and Magnesium,

(and the center not only wouldn't hold

but couldn't exist)

Air vs. Californium,

water versus insect virus.

Remember that He said forgive, not forget.

Into the void we go with a commercial jingle

on our lips.

They thought rock 'n roll would change the world

And now it sure enough sells

laxatives, automobiles and various excreta,

while we lie through our mobile phones.

Government officials have been doing

some serious soul-searching.

So far they've found nothing.

Our latest line wastes profitably

and our wires are invisibly thin.

There are lots of folks here

just like me:

I'm only a bourgeois refugee.

"we need fewer fuckers on the planet!"

Reproductive skills are not always adaptive.

We need more sadhus, searchers, saints,

barrenesses and impotentates.
"This Petro-Park will never last;
we're the wave of the past,"
A very few awfully ancient angel-hipsters
had even wandered down from the mountains
to find that we now have women warriors to deploy
and maps thet show neither old Babylon
nor New Babylon.

(1990)

# REUNION

It's the Full Grass Moon
    and we're mired here in maya –
  Now the subtle rains begin.
    I'm trying to read the signs.
        They say timing is crucial –
      With you, my timing is simple,
                is always.
The Pink Flower Moon illumines the face
        of *mi compañera* of True North.
         we discuss the world of dust.
          Together we are celebation:
            The stranger who loves
like kin,
              the fire that we
might have been!
  From opposite banks of the river we wave;
      You with an Ace,
        And I but a knave.
   we've each been the meal that predators crave.
     (We've all been foolish
         and a few of us brave.)

Dragons won't come when you summon
>   And you can't hear the songs that bats sing.
>      The future is where dreams live
>         (to the present they flock)
>      The past is a graveyard of dreams
>                                    it seems.
>      Parts of the imaginary and parts of the real
>            are not visible to you.
>                           And parts are.
>   May we stay alive long enough
>                        to be
>                     what we
> might have been.

(1991)

# DISPERSALVATION

Birds of stone fly to the bottom of the lake.
All I hear are voices
and some of them are mine.
Sometimes I have the brains of a slug,
And sometimes I see God.
Come here and sit by the fire, love.
Let's feed our names to the flames.
Burning dogs bark at empty trains.
The money-sick bastards who rule us
think they're carving up the pie.
These creatures already dead think they may never die.
Sheer paucity of imagination
has brought on audacity and usurpation.
All of the interstate pirates have crashed your
mother's party.
Neon ponies vanish in a hot pink flash.
The world's latest Roman dogs
(The oligarch, His Chief Spy and His Top Cop)
dish out videopiates to the masses.
Their mantra is "growth, profit, pleasure."

Everybody's One True Friend made love to the executioner's only child

(who couldn't conceive of it).

Descendants of the dictator organized erotic miscreants.

The lesser of two evils was looking fine;

A prophet spoke loud with no words.

The children sought music, love and poetry.

They got liberty and death.

Everyone's sure they have the answer,

None can put it in plain words.

We're looking for the same people

who led us into this morass

to lead us out.

The amoral power elite

investigates its own malignancy

and finds innocence:

another day at the office –

all of the biggest corporations

have bought the most beautiful people

to assure us that they're saving the earth.

Making craters out of molehills is no better.

There stood a young woman

with a stone in her hand,

in the territories where no breath was safe.

Gregorian Rock on the radio

wails about its Super
Power hormones.

Mass media, murderers of grammar,

seduce the post-literate with mantra of

"more, mine, myopia."

Golden platitudes reach new altitudes –

The Lord High Bean-Counter

blithely bypasses survival opportunities.


I have no tribe left here –

they must have all died of shame.

Storm clouds are gathering, darlin',

C'mon in out of the pain.

The troubadour of trouble has arrived:

Drunks are singing in the rain.

The new man and new woman

will arise as clay –

No heroes, no heroines,

come a new day.

No leaders to fail,

No demigods to hail.

Your upper-middlebrow angst

is gonna seem awfully silly

as the empire crumbles about your eyes.


Stone birds try in vain to fly.

There are limits even to the sky.

Light flies agley and the world grows dark.

The exile's last hope is a child's fresh heart:

Nothing so precious as an earthly breath.

Dogs sniff at the edges of a burning lake.

The conjurer is never what she seems,

Everybody's One True Love embraces an angel of death –

Gather sparks, rebuild the beam.

(1991)

Philip Finkle

# PASTORLAE PAST

Queen Anne's lace and chicory
                line the road to our past history.
        There is wonder all around –
                        we mistake it for just ground.
    You're high-strung and I'm low-key.
                we were never sure just what to do.
        You spoiled me for anyone else,
                And I ruined me for you.
    In daylight we sketched smoky schemes,
                By night we searched each other's seams:
        scars left by bad gambles, revolving losses with no
handles.
    I looked deep into your eyes
                and thought I saw us: destiny.
    I watched you turn and walk away
                        and learned synchronicity.
        Ever since the crash it's been no fun.
    After all these years I'm quite good at one.
    We're older now, it won't be long.
        Cicadas' pulse anchors the song;
                Crickets' licks join in the tune:

The insect world jams with the moon.

I'm the one on whom you can depend –

where does the wind start?

where does time end?

I can't remember my dreams.

I can't forget your face.

we walked through chicory and Queen Anne's lace.

(1991)

# POETIC JUSTICE

Let the many become the few,
  Now its another turndown day
      Here in the land of the brew and the home of the
fey –
          The battle of poets is not visionary.
              It is academic.
          Archivists of anger, on the cusp,
                  soon to be dust,
                  How many-thorned thy rose?
  we know all of the old stories;
      we crave the undomesticated new –
          we have muddy thoughts and lots of isms.
            we have little hope and many prisons.
  Won't you please tell me, Pilot –
      are we heavenbound or forlorn?
  why do we keep settling for the least possible world?
          Have we lost the sidereal rhythm to our flesh-
driven rhyme?
      I met a fire with her eyes,
          I've never known those ties that bind,
              I recognize neither you nor your disguise.
              we're each so human and no one's pure.

Life's so short and nothing's sure.

It's true there was a woman once.

Her heart was wide and her mind was lean.

I might have been the longest shot in town;

She was the best thing I'd ever seen.

She still had good luck charms and daydreams;

I didn't seem to fit in anywhere.

I wove poverty grass and larkspur

into a wreath that she refused to wear in

her hair.

(1992)

# ADAM SMITH, PLEASE CALL HOME

They way we love is killing us,
>    You've only heard the small birds sing.
> The way we live's not fulfilling us,
>    Have you seen the raptor on the wing?
> Even our music lies to us
>          about deviate license and cheap thrills.
>       Four-legged meets two-legged face-to-face,
>          Respect turns to disgust.
>       Big wheel runs by grace,
>             Little wheel turns on trust.
> Wolf-Poet walks on al fours and begs on two;
>       Prays to the full moon and wails to the new.
>    He dreamt he saw himself on TV
>             voting for the medium candidate:
> worshipping the gods of consumption, praising men
of great presumption –
>             There is a madman dancing in the rain,
> All because a certain woman can't recall his name.
> The girl in the gourd-mask is now dressed in red.
>    A man with no backbone offers his head.
> Golden blood of the Sun, Silver tears of the Moon:
>          Big wheel turn,

little wheel spin.

Dealer hits you again,

once again.

A childless woman carrying a burning loaf of bread,

searches a dry creek bed

for the slightest dog-scent of

any living god.

Former fiduciary queens,

dealing in commodities of comfort,

rule derelict sycophants.

In the backstreets of our old-growth cities

we toast the golden age of boils and poxes:

the glorious running sores and

festering wounds

of profitable gashes in the earthbreast.

It's the old story:

The gentle crushed,

The arrogant enriched.

Capitalism's Ghost Dance

can't bring back the unsullied resources.

She-wizard worked the complex calculus of sex.

Dog-Soldiers manipulated the simple abacus of

finance.

The big ones gulp the meat,

The little ones gnaw the bones.

Wolf-Poet watched the girl in the green dress

    put on her clay mask and tavern feathers to wear
to the dance.
    The sweet grass widow and her rabbit child,
        ears twitching at the tocsin call of a toxic pall,
        wondered at the plunder and huddled for heat –
            To the victor remains what's spoiled.
            Love is always young,
                Revenge is seldom sweet.
                Master of linear space,
                Emeritus of inner disgrace –
                Time is money to you. . . . . .
                But then isn't everything?

                    (1993)

# NOW THAT THE CARNIVAL'S LEFT TOWN

A three-legged dog with a mouth full of feathers
　　limps towards a home too fine for a lowly cur.
　Now we don't care;
　　　　　we've seen it all,
　　　　　　naked to the waste –
　　　　　The sow's purse is all ears.
　　　　Youth is the learning of capacities;
　　　　　Maturity is the learning of limitations –
　　　　　　Your matter has assumed
　　　　　　　the costume of my heart.
　　　　　Now you have nothing left to teach,
　　　　You must just practice what you preach,
　　　The squeakiest wheel has way too much grease –
　　　　what's good for all is good for each.
　If we wanted less we could have more.
Sometimes you can feel when you just can't think.
　I've suckled for survival
　　　　at the techno-industrial teat
　　　　　　hanging from the beast's belly.
camelot-visions of man-centered nature.
　　　　　Be Gone!

Pharaohs had their tombs;
                Presidents build libraries.
        Avarice and arrogance
                now try to learn the Sun Dance.
                Corporate-capitalism craves a vacuum –
                Thus it devours everything!
        where there is evil afoot in the world
                        its name is Man.
        All of the blondes with their tortured hair
                        offered vapors and flames –
        But I couldn't recognize their favorite songs,
                I didn't know their dark-maned names –
        In for a dime,
                        in for a dollar.
        She said,
                "Happy endings aren't endings;
                        only happy moments."
        Exactly half a moon hangs in the evening sky.
        Less than half a chance remains
                                of salvaging her hart.
                And I want only to hold her
                        and forget morning.

                                            (1993)

# IN THE LAND OF THE ONE-EYEDS

Blesséd are the blind.
  Half-blessed are we.
      we've had Plenty for free.
  Here,
      gangsters are heroes while the humble are
despised.
      we chase the easy buck,
          Hoping for the lottery-millionaire's luck;
              or searching for that roller-coaster fuck –
                  a hit of the good stuff,
                      the big thrill and a cheap giggle.
  Commerce and fashion are our truest passions.
      Our new Golden Rule:
          Always stimulate demand;
              Always demand stimulation.
      we build such elaborately beautiful theories,
          which we then drive aground on such ordi-
nary rocks.
      For us,
          the stars,
              like aged hookers,

> > forced to hang out under the glare of sodium

vapor lamps,

> > at the corner of Desperado and Seven-

teenth

> > > are poems painted on black velvet.


The One-Eyeds forgot
  that the Holy Goof must first be holy
> > > and only secondarily goofy.
But still
> there was the smell of sweetgrass burning
> > and the sound of songs of human yearning –
The Lesser of Two Evils
> > > sashayed its finest stuff
> > Past the Law of Diminishing returns.
> Being fitted for a straitjacket is a snap!
Man pontificates'
> > Woman proliferates –
> > > Ceremony is the harvest of structure.
> Those Old-Timers who paired for once,
> > together for alltime in a long slow desire,
> > > Admired   eagles   and   others   of   their

feather:

> > Together through the thin and the thick,
> > > Even unto death,
> > > > slow or quick.

All these afflictions of the heart

                                are just rehearsals

           for that final dance of departure. . .

                     The arrow covets the archer.

                              (1994)

# NO MENOS, NO MÁS

The Maya discovered Zero instead of the wheel.
Their polulation was reduced from 70 million
                                    to less than 4 million
            in just 150 years of
                        "European cultural influence."
            Now amoral corporate hustlers
                    extol the binary benefits of cybertopia.
                        For lack of a song,
                                homogenized globalization claims
the future.
                        Somewhere in this world
                        there's one enormously rich Joe
                            without the slightest paradigm
but "Mine",
                            cranking up his media-minions
dreamdrive.
                            And he's handing out differently
colored hats
                            named  Corporation-This  and
CEO-That,
                            President of Presumption
                                and Prince of Plenty –

Darlin'

        are you bored on the Superhighway of Disin-
formation?

        Your rich Yankee Uncle promises all of the latest
machinery

            and some Japanese to run it.

    There's a fossil-burning flock of fools

        traipsing down the idiot-proof Interstate.

        The hottest new product in consumer-
dupedom

            is the "soundtrack-backpack" –

            makes every pedestrian life a movie!

Rich Fortress America vs.

              Poor Hope of the Streets –

Omnipotent transnationals devour their opposition.

    New is Better.

        The Aberrant claim the headlines –

        Everyday we witness the Rites of Excess.

    A few poets are just trying to salvage love –

    But then,

            "Them ain't poets!

                Them's perfessors –

              training soldiers of con-
sumption,

            with their meter,

                their metier

and their moral matter."

Meanwhile the bands are setting up

           on the easy side of town.

      where there's no true love

        there's lots of sub-love to be found.

    Even the linear-minded

          come full circle.

It's easier to believe in nothing

       than to practice anything.

(1996)

# SHE WAS A PIRATE IN AN AGE OF SHIPWRECK

The first time I met her was in the Chinaman's kitchen.

She sipped golden seal and mushroom soup.

She chants, she encants –

"Do everything a little,

Don't do anything a lot."

There she stood determined,

one-directional like time;

reckless like history –

not like mystery:

multidirectional.

what sort of music does a savage beast make?

"Males do best as birds (think plumage).

They're most effective *en masse* (as witness armies and sperm).

For a while she lived with some starving autist,

mostly as a weight-loss scheme

and a chance to do a little modelling –

Her indiscretion grew up to become her glory.

She became mastress of the herbal heal.

She always had some kif to share,

with which to weave a wondrous spell

to lift one from the depths of hell

or just relieve a minor pain,

and there's the bind:

Blind and mindless is the curse that binds.

Where do you put the money in??

Where does the music come out?

She once ran a game in the carny;

She used to sing in the bars.

She knew when to keep her mouth shut;

She drove someone else's car.

Her life was a fiction,

like sex without friction.

worked herself into a trick groove,

demimonde of a crafty art.

She went out to comfort an old flame and got burned:

charged with felony-possession of a vegetable.

She did some time

and now there she stands without a man,

Soon to lose her electric kid,

wearing his mystic earring and transcendental hair:

Video-Emperor of the Mall,

A rune, a glyph, a symbol, a myth.

Too old to die young;

too scarred to live dumb.

"Yes, your uniform of dust is quite fetching,

                far   from   the   smell   of

institutional food."

The last time I saw her was in some corner cafe.

Her every laugh ended in a cough –

She's seen enough.

She had suicide-eyes that bind

and a tight-lipped smile that unwinds like a bro-
ken watch.

she quaffs the last of her *yerba maté.*

It's Daylight's-Savings-Time-Eve

and later than you think.

(1996)

# METAPHYSTICUFFS

There are limits to the limitless.

Some will pass and some will pour –

Some have less and some have more.

"I just want to be with you," he said.

"I want you to bear my devil-child."

She said, "Well this changes everything."

"But," she added, "this changes nothing."

By the time she'd become "the New woman",

he was no longer a young man.

It was the summer solstice –

The yuccas were riotously abloom.

The alleys were full of hollylocks and lightning bugs

and old dogs whose times were near.

Mimosa blossoms look as strange as the neighbors,

the cicada chorus harmonized.

Just because the digilectuals can count in gigas we let them steer.

Meta-capitalism keeps constantly growing its power-grid.

In modern warfare the weapons have become the heroes.

The binarati cut and dry the flower of our future.

God is a possibility, not a certainty.

The near-sighted visionary and the obese vegetarian plot rebellion.

The god of certainty is unscientific.

A possible god evolves.

(1997)

# UNREQUITED REQUISITE

"The same sun that brings out the snake,
brings out the lily."

- Uncle Joe Cannon

We're telling each other our same old stories again,
        but in their latest versions.
      (I worked on the railroad, you soared on the great
winds.)
   You're lecturing me again on the nature of sand (life's
or love's).
        "Get a fix on it and it shifts."
     I sermonize on time's relentless flow:
        "when we end, it lifts."
      I'm only a jr. assistant weasel –
        Just another sorry cipher in some mean-
ingless capitalist scheme.
          My excuse?
        Hey, it ain't no life, but its a living.
        Fast cars and easy money.
     I've got no home page and I'm lost out on the
highway –

Because I owe the government some money for breaking a rule

And because I owe the government some money for obeying a rule.

You're but a bit of flesh.

I'm but a short rush of air.

I'm a piece of meat that sings.

You're the short-order cook for my grilled-cheese life.

where there is no right there things go wrong.

where all is fright there can be no song –

A movie star with a transmissable disease,

A meditator without ease.

I can't get you out of my dreams.

I can't get you into my life.

I'm not ready to die. I'm not finished with flesh.

Oh, all the many saints of India – Rise Up!

we know more than the past

but less than the future.

(1997)

# CONTEXTS/YOUTH

## Drumbeat 1

In 1945 Ho Chi Minh declared Vietnam's independence from its French colonialist rulers. Two and one half billion dollars of U.S. aid did nothing to forestall the overwhelming of French forces by the Viet Minh in 1954 at Dien Bien Phu. The resulting Geneva Peace Conference provisionally divided Vietnam into north and south, to be reunited by an election in 1956. It was common knowledge that in a free and open election Ho Chi Minh would win in a landslide. President Eisenhower refused to allow the election and threw support to the puppet Saigon regime of Ngo Dinh Diem, a Catholic in a Buddhist country. Near the end of 1959 there were 760 "military advisors" to the 243,000 South Vietnamese Armed Forces. A Viet Cong attack on Bien Hoa brought the first two U.S. military casualities of the war.

## Interlude 1

Ten days after the French surrender at Dien Bien Phu, Thurgood Marshall's victory was handed down by the Supreme Court in Brown vs. Board of Education, calling for the racial integration of public schools.

In 1957 Elizabeth Eckford of the "Little Rock Nine" marched through a sea of white faces contorted by hatred and hurling curses and at the end of the day at Little Rock High School she returned home to wring the spit from her dress.

Automobile-empowered Neal Cassidy sped down the twisting American highway spieling his head-bobbing, hipster bop beat jive stoned "Go!" monologue – tapping time to radio, windshield wiper, tire-hum rhythym.

Black folks had the music, white folks had the money. In Memphis, Tennessee, Sam Phillips found a pretty white boy who "sounded black" when he sang – let the rock 'n roll adolescent marketing begin!

The mass-marketing of birth control pills liberated women from biological determinism; separating sex from reproduction and pleasure from consequence.

Puritanical censorship tried to muffle D.H. Lawrence, James Joyce, Henry Miller, J.D. Salinger and dropped plums in the laps of Lenny Bruce and Hugh Hefner.

Sputnik spooked us!

The Cold War-conceived Interstate Highway System increased fossil fuel consumption, further bled the railroads, metastisized suburban sprawl, sliced through ancient animal migratory routes, helped homogenize popular culture and promoted transportation by personal vehicle.

Allen Ginsburg cruised the streets of revolutionary Havana, startling *los barbudos* – the revolution for individual freedom meets the socio-economic revolution.

Television adds to the uniformity of pop culture and leads to the truest American art-form: the TV commercial, and to the explosion of celebrity-culture.

## Drumbeat 2

In January 1961, John F. Kennedy took office with 900 U.S. military personnel in Vietnam. In 1963 American television viewers were subjected to the sight of self-immolation by Buddhist monks protesting their treatment by Diem's regime. Disagreement over conduct of the war also contributed to the CIA's concurrence in the assasination of Diem in a military coup. Three weeks after Diem's assasination came Kennedy's: it was November 1963 and there were 16,300 American troops in Vietnam. In August 1964 Kennedy's successor, Lyndon Johnson distorted the Gulf of Tonkin incident into a major attack on U.S. naval vessels, requiring retaliation. In the ensuing Naval air attacks North Vietnamese forces shot down two Navy aircraft and took their first American P.O.W. when Johnson was hounded from office in 1968 U.S. troop strength stood at 536,000 – 30,600 had been killed in action.

## Interlude 2

Rosa Parks refused to give up her seat on the bus; Martin Luther King Jr. led the Montgomery bus boycott.

In 1963 in Bull Connor's Birmingham, segregationists blew up four young girls in their Bible class.

In 1964 (as the Gulf of Tonkin escalation was going on) the FBI, after a long search, dug the bodies of Andrew Goodman, James Chaney and Michael Schwerner out of an earthen dam in Mississippi. They'd traveled there to help register black voters which the Ku Klux Klan had judged punishable by torture and death.

In "bourgeois-retirement-Florida" it's "Good night, Dr. Sax"....at 47, Jack Kerouac, King of the Beats, died a raging alcoholic death.

Cassius Clay became Muhammed Ali; Dylan went electric and turned the Beatles on to pot; Timothy Leary hopscotched the country's campuses preaching his LSD-gospel of "Turn On, Tune In, Drop Out."

A sequined, bloated, Vegas-Elvis turned on to a different tune and dropped out at age 42. The King is dead.

Youth culture proved a philosophical bust but a great commercial success.

Covert chickens roosting: Patrice Lumumba assasinated in the Congo – Democratically ruling Iranian Prime Minister Mohammad Mossadeq toppled, resulting in the installation of the shah – 1954 CIA operation in Guatamela results in the overthrow of democratically elected Jacobo Arbenz – In 1967, Che Guevara, revolutionary icon, tracked down with CIA technology, captured by Bolivian forces, executed, trophy hands cut off, body hidden – with U.S. encouragement in 1973, democratically elected Chilean President Salvador Allende overthrown by the military with numerous leftists tortured, killed, disappeared.

Television brought the nobility of the civil rights struggle and the horrors of Vietnam into American livingrooms.

In 1968, in Memphis, Tennessee Martin Luther King Jr., apostle of non-violence was gunned down by the forces of hate.

Drumbeat 3

In 1969 Richard Nixon took office; by June U.S. troop strength peaked at 543,000. The policy of "Vietnamization of the war" was replacing GI's with ARVIN troops.

Inten-sive bombing of Laos and Cambodia was kept secret and then justified as disrupting supply lines along the Ho Chi Minh trail. The military's image was further degraded by the public exposure of the My Lai massacre. Ho Chi Minh died in 1969. In 1970 Henry Kissinger began secret peace talks in Paris. In 1972 Nixon was re-elected with the promise of "a secret plan to end the war" and the inept anti-war campaign of George McGovern. Nixon's secret squad of "plumbers" were caught breaking into Democratic headquarters at the Watergate, beginning the unraveling of Tricky Dick. 1973 brought the end of the draft, the release of 590 American POW's, further withdrawal and limiting of U.S. combat troops. South Vietnamese armed forces totalled 1,110,000 (223,748 KIA's). In August 1974 Nixon avoided impeachment by resigning. In 1975 the NVA captured Hue, Danang and Saigon – End of war; April 30, 1975 –

U.S. war dead: 58,000 (all of whose names would be carved into a black granite wall

in Washington, D.C.)

Enemy losses: 3,600,000 (no wall).

(2000)

# PARTIAL PHILOSOPHY AND COMPLETE SEX

Baruch Spinoza, 17th century Jew –
   banished by the Orthodox Amsterdam community...\
      yet to maintain intellectual independence
                           refused academic post
               and made his living by grinding lenses.
   Spinozan thought:
               The world exists as a necessary result of
               God's attainment of a state of perfection.


The smell of you in my nose,
      The taste of you on my tongue.
   The curve of you on my fingertips,
         Your essence on my lips,
               Your face in my eyes
                  Your ache in my thighs
                     Your soul in my heart
                           Your earth-anchored thought –
                  My mouth memorizing your mouth;
               Your geometric demonstration of my linear
fate.
                  We're bound by symmetry,
                           not to mention biology –


                                 Q.E.D.


   Spinozan thought:

Intuitional knowledge is attained
as a result of
some   understanding   of   the
nature of God.

(2000)

# PAST VOICE PRESENT

It was the Crow Moon when you called.
  winter's grip had just loosened.
        so much of love consists of lost causes.
  Now its the Year of the Horse again
              (twice since we were together).
        Perhaps modern love is just
              the desire for what cannot be –
        Ideas (wishes for the impossible)
              chasing actual flesh.


I am an old man now,
    with no mother and no child.
  I can't keep from crying in the movies –
          sometimes I remember to kneel
                but forget how to pray.
        Sleep is a foreign country
                in which I cannot stay long.
        Count me in or count me out.
            Help me sing or let me shout.
  All of the so-called adults
    arc cating milkduds and watching vampire movies.

Alone is not the same as lonely –
But I wish I could lie
               once again in your arms.

                   (2001)

# CAVEAT EMPTOR

we live in a modern version of the Roman Empire,
 but with lots more bread and way more circuses –
  Our commercial global Goliaths peddle their
scams offshore.
   Our concerns both middle-class and impe-
rial
    (rendered unto Caesar),
   Our soldiers eager to annihilate myriad blips
on a screen:
     Arcade wars to make the world safe for
our technologies.
  We're still nostalgic for the Old God of Vengeance –
   Thousands of eyes for an eye,
    Thousands of teeth for a tooth.
     Billions for revenge instead of peace.
  Nearly everyone else in the world
    thinks that our House of Cards is a wondrous
mansion.
     Neocapitalism is a pyramid scheme:
      living in finity, betting on infinity.
       Information is not comprehension.
    Our constant goals: profit and control –

we have all of the tools but little of the good will required for adaptation.

Diversity is the best evolutionary strategy

(corporations have mastered an illusory diversity).

The man who said, "what you don't know won't hurt you"

was killed by a stranger.

You wanna be safe? You wanna be free?

-Choose one.

There is a story each of us is to tell with our life –

For most it's the story of our children;

For some of us it's the story of our dreams.

Science is the study of God's material manifestations.

Older now, we're waiting for more shoes to drop,

with tools of killing and tools of commerce.

(If you think its lonely at the top you should try it at the bottom.)

Me,

I'll have my usual caviar and peanutbutter sandwich.

How to spark a revolt against comfort and ease

(under glorious skies of bourgeois wonder)/

The birds know

what I can only guess.

I can fly through the air on my most frivolous
whim.

They are launched on a mission of survival.

They look for food or escape from death –
I search for amusement or escape from boredom.

The Alpha Male scratches himself

and wanders circularly

in the Mall that's become America.

After the worst imaginable happens –

what do we call what goes wrong after that?

say some pretty words now, pilgrim.

Extinction is crouched just in front of you.

(2001)

# AFTER PATCHEN

No,
  I haven't been saving myself for her –
    I've been spending myself
        oh so judiciously,
            oh so prodigiously,
                oh so hopelessly.

I have a warm room
  and a comfortable bed
      and a surfeit of books and music
          and a window on the world.
              There is nothing more needed
                  for simple contentment –

But she is well provided for
  and still beautiful
      and I am invisible.

(2003)

# ALL GOOD

I turned on the tube
  just to watch the pols bob and weave.
    I swear to god, darlin' –
      I never thought that you'd leave.
    Daddy came home from his war a hero.
      The best we got from ours was zero.
    When I was young I bragged.
      "You know I'm good at travelling light –
        Light's all I've got
          and I'm trying to shed that."
      The Laureate entered –
        a tenured professor in a necktie.
          (never trust a used car salesman
wearing bluejeans).
        The eighty year old poet
              finally finished his only epic
          and sighed some mild relief –
            Lonelier than a hermit's funeral.
    The Minister for Rapid Exhaustion
        of Non-Renewable Resources
      pronounced time a one-way street.
    The Secretary of Commercial Exploitation
          leapt to his feet with applause.
  "All I know is what I read in the newspapers"

is a long way from
    "I believe what I see on TV" –
        where only the prettiest faces
            bring us the ugliest news.


They're selling death and gasolene.
    We're paying taxes for their wars.
      We may have overstayed our welcome:
        Overconsuming and living too long.
      Out in the burbdocks:
        Cyberscum, techno-creeps
          clogging up the lanes
        Ad-mad and fantasy foolish –
    Down on the corporate farm
      there is no pony just for riding.
    Old people in the supermarket
      are poking packages of meat,
        as if to test the feeling of dead flesh.
Do I hear "crumble-down economics"?
    Or maybe its just one of those mornings,
      I stumble to work
        not particularly proud of my species.
A bald woman keeps walking in and out of the room
      in search of her eyebrows.
Now the birds conspire against us
    with viruses to arrest our unchecked reign.
      They fly in the face of arrogance.

      Do you think this microbial dance is happen-
stance?
   Out on a cold winter sidewalk
      a man huddled over his cigarette,
         wearing a salon tan,
            is arguing over a cell phone
               with his soon-to-be-ex-wife
                  over   custody   of   the   frozen
embryos.
   All of the niche marketers
      are lined up in the mall
         like an econo-firing squad.
  Now its May in January
  And December in April.
      she was trying to make the scene
         when there wasn't one left
            (whales are committing suicide
               as we fill the oceans with carbon
dioxide).
  Sure,
   we'll pretend to be emperor
      though we've not a stitch on,
         walking through the Middle East
            where all must be covered.

                       (2004)

# REMNANTS AND PENANCE

As-Salámn 'Alaykum
    (Peace be unto you)


The deluded versus the excluded –
  our overpaid Hessians
     battle their paradise-bound martyrs.
  Our warriors ride into the fray
       blaring heavy metal goth rock (death of the
cool).
         God save us or damn us.


I remember when "the movement"
    was always in the background music
     and spring was in my step.
  Now a surgeon has removed my swagger
    and a shrink suppressed my palaver,
      while madmen rule the country yet
    and corn that could be fed to the world's starving
      feeds our insatiable engines instead.


I go to drop my last dime
       into a pay phone

(to call her)

and it says,

"50 cents now brother –

ain't you got no cell?"

Late for the shape-shifters' convention,
  now I'm wandering empty streets so lost.
    Smile in the sunshine feels good.
      At ten below I start feeding
                        stray cats in the alley.
            where is the new rebel?
              There must be a new rebel. . . . .
                we surely can't settle
                  for this kettle empty of fish.

The president starts awake in a cold night sweat
  at the globalized industrialman-made
      mass species extinction underway in his rule.
        (only a zoo-ful of DNA on file
            and a seedbank account underground.)
  Two wings of one political party
    offer a fork in the road
            that leads back to a merger –
        The illusion of choice to sustain us:
          This modern twitch,
            'This imperial itch.

well-oiled Washington
blood-blinded in Babylon.


wa' Alaikum As-Salám
(And peace be unto you).

(2007)

# WINTER

I.

Tick, tick – clock counting
drip, drip – icicles meltimg
sun thaws each day's art

II.

Moon through bare branches:
chiaroscurist at work –
winter shadows dance!

# SPRING

III.

Morning dew on grass
white blooms of serviceberry
new chorus, old song

IV.

Breeze through the window
train whistle in the distance
- destination dreams

# SUMMER

### V.

Fireflies blink their code
    at dusk – questioning where are
            butterflies sleeping?

### VI.

Footsteps approaching
    squirrel darts up and behind tree –
        cautious evader!

# AUTUMN

### VII.

Red, orange, yellow –
    recite the midwestern leaves:
        celebrate wonder!

### VIII.

Leaf falls – can you hear?
        hummingbird migrates – hurry!
        wind chimes sing motion

(2007)-

# ON CALLING ON OLD FLAME

You had the full fire then –
  where has that flame now gone?
    Are you sheltering the spark inside?
      Are you searching for the ark?
        The machinery's breakin' down
                all around us and within.
          we,
                  once young, lean, so hungry;
                      now sated and dim.
                    Been that, done there;
                  seen where, begat naught.
            Keep the chatter short,
              let the verse go long –
Make the coffee and the women strong,
    Serve the tea too hot and the beer too cold,
              My friends still young when old.
          Delivery first, promises last.
        Kisses slow, true words never past.
                  Laughter easy, hatred hard –
            Expect by the inch, forgive by the yard.
I remember the smile in your eyes

and the light on your lips,

that laser beam look

and that saber sharp wit.

what's the skinny on the pall?

what free bear still awes us all?

Rain till it floods, drought till its bones –

Brother Frog, Sister Swallow so long.

The real never ending, life bringing grief.

The gift of clear reason,

the pure sigh of relief.

I was crazy too often.

You've been distant too long.

I've been solved as a cipher.

You will seem as a song.

(2007)